a cat

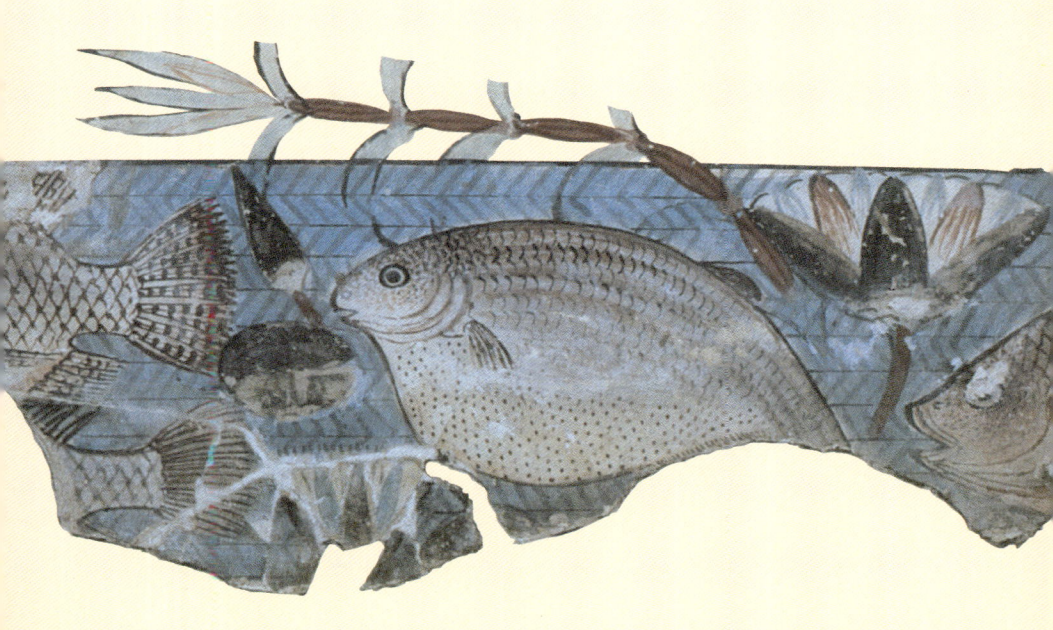

some fish

lots of birds

four butterflies

a girl

This painting is called *Hunting in the Marshes*.

The man's name is Nebamun.

About the painting

Hunting in the Marshes was painted on a wall in Egypt more than three thousand years ago. Parts of the painting fell off and were lost long ago. We do not know the name of the artists who painted it.

The painting is now in the Egyptian rooms at the British Museum in London.